SPILLING THE SWEET TEA

presents

All About The Jam

COOKBOOK

WRITTEN BY
CARLENA DAVIS

PHOTOGRAPHY BY
EBES OLUMESE & CARLENA DAVIS

"
TO MY MOTHER,
AS A TOKEN OF MY
GRATITUDE
FOR TEACHING ME
ALL ABOUT THE JAM.
"

CONTENTS

A LETTER FROM CARLENA

Welcome to my "All about the Jam" recipe collection. I'm delighted to share with you the many ways that you can incorporate jam into any dish from an appetizer, to an entree and even a cocktail.

I am a Southern girl and a busy working mom who started a food blog back in 2017. I wanted to "Spill the Sweet Tea" on how to make great Southern dishes and share some quick thirty minute meals for busy working moms. I was taught how to cook and make homemade preserves by my mom. I say all the time that there would be "no tea to spill" without my mama and all she taught me in the kitchen. For as long as I can remember, I've loved to cook, bake, and share recipes with my friends and family. My food blog Spilling the Sweet Tea is my way to sharing my family recipes and my love for Southern food.
I appreciate you purchasing my recipe collection, and coming to "get the tea" on great dishes that incorporate my homemade jam.

I can't wait for you to try these recipes and I hope you enjoy them as much as my family have enjoyed them!

With lots of love,
Carlena

OUR JAM

RASPBERRY

Our raspberry preserves has one key ingredient that brings out the fruity essence of the raspberry which is Chambord liqueur. We use fresh raspberries and a small amount of Chambord liquor in addition to sugar to make our raspberry preserves. The combination of the three gives you the most robust flavor of the fruit and the perfect balance of sweet and tartness.

BLACKBERRY

Our blackberry jam is the perfect addition to your charcuterie board this holiday season. We use fresh blackberries, fresh lemon juice, and butter in addition to sugar to make our blackberry preserves. Our blackberry jam is not seedless which is intentional because blackberry seeds are full of Vitamin C, K and hgh in fiber.

PEACH

Our peach preserves manages to capture the sweetness of fresh peaches but also offer a homemade quality that reminds you of your grandmother's kitchen. We use North Carolina and Georgia peaches in our preserves and only three other ingredients that allows you to enjoy summer's favorite fruit year round.

NUTRIONAL FACTS AND STATS

Raspberries serve as a very good source of fiber. They are also low in calories and fat, cholesterol-free and high in fiber and vitamin C, raspberries are a heart-healthy food.

Peaches are a super healthy addition to your daily diet. They're low in calories—only 60 calories in each cup—and they're a great source of fiber, potassium and vitamins A and C.

Blackberries have been shown to improve cognitive and motor skills. Blackberries also contain vitamin A, which supports the immune system, which combats infections and illness.

SOUTHERN CHARCUTERIE BOARD WITH

Spilling the Sweet Tea Jam

READY IN 30 MIN   **SERVES 8-10**

They are great for special occasions or just fun as an appetizer before dinner. I am calling this a Southern Style Charcuterie Board because I used some of my favorite products that are made in North Carolina. I adore being from the South and love to highlight some of the amazing food products that are made there. In order to make a charcuterie board, you only need some creativity, a large cutting board or cheese board and some of your favorite cheeses, smoked meats, crackers and some sweet and savory items to pair it with.

ITEMS USED ON THE SOUTHERN CHARCUTERIE BOARD

Trader Joe's Blue Stilton Blue Cheese
Trader Joe's Taste of Inspirations
Brie Round Cheese
Trader Joe's Chevre Creamy Fresh Goat Cheese
Trader Joe's Columbus Calabrese Salimi
Trader Joe's Gourmet Pepperoni
Trader Joe's Fig and Olive Crisps
Trader Joe's Candied Pecans
Trader Joe's Dried Apricots
Trader Joe's Italian Breadsticks
Trader Joe's Baby Black Grapes
Trader Joe's Brioche Toast

Blackberry Jam
Raspberry Preserves
Mild Hoop Cheese
Mt. Olive Hot Okra
Mt. Olive Sweet Gherkins
Golden Farms Honey

Other Items- Raw Almonds, fresh blackberries, crostini, olives, and rosemary springs.

TIPS

Use the tutorial video below as a guide to make your southern charcuterie board.
https://www.youtube.com/watch?v=nEIr9TKRiYk

SPILLING THE
SWEET TEA
Homemade Blackberry
Jam

A scone is a single-serving cake or quick bread originating in the United Kingdom. American scones are often dense wedges or triangles, while British scones are taller and usually round.

Blackberry JAM STUFFED SCONES

READY IN **45 MIN** SERVES **4-5**

INGREDIENTS

2 cups of all-purpose flour

1/4 cup of white sugar

2 teaspoons of baking powder

1/4 teaspoon of salt

1 stick of cold unsalted butter, cubed

1 large egg, slightly beaten

1 teaspoon of vanilla extract

1/2 cup of heavy cream

1/4 cup of Blackberry Jam

DIRECTIONS

Preheat your oven to 400 degrees F. Line a baking sheet with parchment paper. In a large bowl, whisk together the flour, sugar, baking powder and salt. Cut the butter into the flour mixture with a pastry blender or two knives. The mixture should look like coarse crumbs. In a bowl whisk the cream with the beaten egg and vanilla. Add this mixture to the flour mixture. Stir until the flour mixture is moistened and a dough is starting to form. Do not over mix. Transfer to a lightly floured surface and knead dough gently four or five times and then divide the dough in half. Roll each half of the dough into a circle about 8 inches round.

Spread the jam on one round of the dough, leaving about a one-inch border. Brush the border with the egg wash. Then place the second round of dough on top of the jam, gently sealing the edges. Crimp the edges of the dough with a fork. Cut this circle in half, then cut each half into 4 pie-shaped wedges (triangles). Place the scones on the baking sheet. Lightly brush the tops of the scones with an egg wash. Bake for about 18 minutes or until golden brown and a toothpick inserted into the center of a scone comes out clean. Remove from oven and place on a wire rack to cool.

SALMON WITH *Blackberry* SAUCE

Making a sauce out of our blackberry jam is a great compliment to a beautiful piece of salmon. It is easy to turn the sweetness of the jam to a savory compliment to the fish.

- Carlena Davis

READY IN 45 MIN　　**SERVES 4-5**

DIRECTIONS

Preheat oven to 400 degrees.

For sauce, in a small saucepan combine jam, shallots, thyme, mustard, and garlic. Bring to a boil and then reduce the heat, whisking frequently. Simmer, uncovered, about 10 minutes or until sauce has thickened. Remove from heat and keep covered.

Rinse salmon fillets and pat dry. Drizzle with oil and season with salt and pepper to taste. Heat cast iron skillet to medium high heat and place fillets in the skillet skin side down. Cook fish until skin is crispy.

Place skillet in the oven and cook about 15 mins. Flip the fish and cook another 10 mins or until desired doneness.

To serve, spoon about 2 tablespoons of the sauce onto each dinner plate. Top with fish. Serve with lemon wedges and, if desired, fresh blackberries.

INGREDIENTS

2- 6oz salmon fillets cut 1 inch thick

½ cup of Blackberry Jam

2 tablespoons finely chopped shallots

1 teaspoon of fresh thyme, finely chopped

1 teaspoon of Dijon mustard

1 clove of garlic, minced

2 tablespoons avocado oil

Salt and Pepper to taste

Lemon slices to garnish

WHIPPED GOAT CHEESE CROSTINI WITH *Blackberry* JAM

READY IN 30 MIN　　　　**SERVES 4-6**

Need a quick and impressive appetizer for your next dinner party? These whipped goat cheese crostinis are a decadent bite that are sure to be a hit at your next event.

DIRECTIONS

Preheat oven to 400 degrees.

Place crostini's on a baking sheet and drizzle olive oil on each crostini. Add fresh cracked pepper and bake until golden brown.

In a small bowl, add goat cheese and whipped cream cheese and use a hand mixer to mix until well combined.

Remove crostini's from the oven and allow to completely cool.

Top cooled crostini's with whipped goat cheese and then with a bit of the blackberry jam. Garnish with fresh mint and fresh blackberries

INGREDIENTS

1 8oz of goat cheese

1 8oz of Whipped Cream Cheese

Crostini, unbaked or a French baguette cut in 1/2 inch slices

Fresh ground black pepper

Olive Oil

Blackberry Jam

Fresh Mint and Fresh Blackberries to garnish

TIPS　Use the tutorial video below as a guide to make your whipped goat cheese crostini with blackberry jam https://www.youtube.com/watch?v=VS8xgV2-lwc

CROCKPOT MEATBALLS WITH
Blackberry JAM

DIRECTIONS

Preheat oven to 425 degrees

In a large bowl, mix together ground turkey, breadcrumbs, egg, garlic powder and paprika. Season with salt and pepper and mix until combined. Form into small sized meatballs.

On a greased baking sheet, add meatballs and cook until the bottom of the meatballs are browned.

In a small saucepan, add jam, ketchup, hot sauce, ground ginger and pepper and bring to a boil. Whisking constantly until the sauce thickens. The sauce will thicken more as it sits.

Add cooked meatballs to a crockpot and pour sauce on top. Toss until all meatballs are well coated.

Place crockpot on warm until ready to serve.

SERVES **4-6**   READY IN 35 **MIN**

INGREDIENTS

1 lb of ground turkey

1/2 cup of breadcrumbs

1 Egg, lightly beaten

1 teaspoon of garlic powder

1/2 tsp. paprika

Salt and pepper to taste

3/4 cups of Blackberry Jam

1/4 cup of brown sugar

1/4 cup of ketchup

2 teaspoons of hot sauce

1 teaspoon of ground ginger

1/4 teaspoon of pepper

Blackberry JAM BARS

INGREDIENTS

2 cups old fashioned oats

2 cups all-purpose flour

1 1/2 cup packed brown sugar

1 teaspoon baking powder

1/2 teaspoon salt

12 tablespoons butter, cubed

1 cup of Blackberry Jam

1/2 cup of finely chopped walnuts

READY IN 45 MINS   SERVES 4-6

 CONTAINS **NUTS**

DIRECTIONS

Preheat the oven to 350 degrees and line a 9×13 inch baking pan with parchment paper. **Tip-** Grease the bottom of the pan and place the parchment paper on top so the paper goes into the pan with ease. Set aside.

Mix the oats, flour, brown sugar, baking powder, salt and finely chopped walnuts in a large bowl. Using a pastry blender, a fork, or two knives, cut butter into flour mixture until it appears sandy and forms fine crumbs. Press two-thirds of the crumble into the bottom of the prepared baking pan. Bake for 10 minutes.

Remove the crust from the oven and spread the jam over the top. In order to for it to be spreadable, warm the jam in the microwave for a few seconds. Sprinkle the remaining 1/3 streusel over the top of the jam layer; bake for another 25-30 minutes or until the crust is lightly golden brown.

Remove the bars from the oven and cool completely before cutting.

Blackberry RUM COCKTAIL

INGREDIENTS

1 Tablespoon of Blackberry Jam

1 teaspoon sugar

5-6 mint leaves

1 teaspoon honey

2 oz of Malibu Rum

Club soda, to top

DIRECTIONS

Muddle jam, sugar, mint leaves in cocktail shaker until leaves are well-bruised and sugar incorporated well. Add rum, honey and ice to shaker.

Shake well. Pour into glass and top with club soda. Garnish with a lime slice and fresh blackberries.

Raspberry Jam RECIPES

This Raspberry Walnut Baked Brie is so delicious and so easy to make. I really like the combination of raspberries and walnuts and of course pairing it cheese is a win/win. It is served warm with crackers and makes an amazing appetizer for a crowd.

Raspberry WALNUT BAKED BRIE

READY IN **45 MIN**   SERVES **4-5**

CONTAINS **NUTS**

DIRECTIONS

Preheat oven to 400 degrees. Line a baking sheet with aluminum foil and lightly grease with cooking spray.

Lay the puff pastry onto the prepared baking sheet . Scrap off the top layer of the brie cheese and then center the brie wheel onto the pastry. Spread the jam evenly over the top of the Brie. Sprinkle the walnuts atop the jam. Fold the puff pastry over the top of the brie sealing all openings. Brush with egg wash all over the puff pastry.

Bake in preheated oven until the pastry is golden brown, about 30 mins. Let it rest for 10 mins before cutting into the baked brie. Serve with crackers and enjoy.

INGREDIENTS

1 sheet of frozen puff pastry, thawed

1 (8oz) round Brie Cheese

1/3 cup of Raspberry Preserves

2 tablespoons of chopped walnuts

1 egg + 2 tablespoons of water

HOMEMADE POP TARTS WITH
Raspberry PRESERVES

As a mom of a six year old, I am always looking for an easy sweet treat that we can make together. She loves helping her momma bake and these pop tarts were a perfect fit for my mini me to help me make.

-Carlena

READY IN 45 MIN

SERVES 4-5

DIRECTIONS

Preheat oven to 425 degrees. Line baking sheets with parchment paper.

Unroll the pie crusts. Place on a lightly floured work surface and roll the crusts slightly with a rolling pin to square the edges. Use a pizza cutter and cut each crust into 8 equal-sized rectangles. Place about 2 teaspoons of raspberry preserves in the center of 8 squares, and spread the jam out to within 1/4 inch of the edge of the pastry square. Top each with another pastry rectangle, and use a fork to crimp the squares together, sealing in the jam. Move the pop tarts to the lined baking sheets.

Bake in the preheated oven until the edges are lightly golden brown, about 7 minutes. Allow to cool on the baking sheets.

While the pop tarts are baking, stir together confectioners' sugar, milk, and vanilla extract in a bowl to make a spreadable frosting.

Spread icing on completely cooled tarts and top with rainbow sprinkles.

INGREDIENTS

1 package of refrigerated pie crusts

1/4 cup of Raspberry Preserves, divided

2 cups of confectioners' sugar

3 tablespoons of milk

1/2 teaspoon of vanilla extract

Rainbow Sprinkles

Raspberry CHEESECAKE STUFFED FRENCH TOAST

READY IN 1 HR   **SERVES 4-6**

Enjoying a good brunch is in my DNA so it only makes sense to share one of my favorite brunch dishes in this recipe collection.

DIRECTIONS

In a bowl, whisk milk, vanilla, sugar, and cinnamon into the beaten eggs until well blended. Set aside.

Using a large storage bag, crush cereal with a rolling pin into fine crumbs. Pour onto a plate and set aside.

In a separate bowl, mix cream cheese, vanilla and Raspberry Preserves until smooth. Spread cream cheese mixture on a slice of brioche bread and top with another slice of brioche bread to make a sandwich.

Melt butter or use cooking spray over medium heat in a large skillet or griddle.

Dip bread into egg mixture, coating thoroughly. Transfer to plate with cereal crumbs and coat well. Cook until well-browned on both sides, about 5 minutes. Dust with confectioners' sugar and nutmeg. Garnish with fresh raspberries and whipped cream.

Serve immediately.

INGREDIENTS

1 cup of milk

2 tablespoons of vanilla extract plus 1 teaspoon for filling
.

1 cup of white sugar

2 tablespoons of cinnamon

2 eggs, beaten

1/2 cup of Raspberry Preserves

4 ounces of whipped cream cheese

Fresh Raspberries

Brioche Bread, sliced

2 cups of Cinnamon Toast Crunch cereal, crushed

Raspberry JAM BREAD

READY IN 1 HR   **SERVES 4-6**

DIRECTIONS

Preheat the oven to 350 degrees.

Grease a 9x5 loaf pan. In the bowl of a stand mixer, cream together the butter and sugar until light and fluffy. Beat in the egg and vanilla until well combined.

Combine the flour, baking powder, and salt in a small bowl. Add the flour mixture a little at a time to the butter mixture, alternating with the buttermilk. Spread half of the batter into the prepared loaf pan. Top with half of the raspberry jam and swirl with a knife. Add remaining batter to the pan and top with remaining jam. Swirl knife through the batter to create a swirl of jam. Bake for 50-60 minutes or until a toothpick inserted in the center comes out mostly clean. Cool before glazing.

To make the glaze, whisk together the powdered sugar, lemon juice and lemon zest. Add more lemon juice if you'd like the glaze thinner. Drizzle over the bread before cutting.

INGREDIENTS

1/2 cup butter, softened

3/4 cup of sugar

1 egg

2 teaspoons of vanilla extract

2 cups of flour

2 teaspoons of baking powder

1 teaspoon of salt

1/2 cup buttermilk

1/2 cup of Raspberry Preserves

1/2 cup of powdered sugar

1 tablespoon lemon juice

Lemon zest

Raspberry PALMIERS

READY IN 35 **MIN**   SERVES **4-6**

These raspberry palmiers are the perfect sweet treat for the special love in your life.
Palmier hearts are a three ingredient cookie that is rolled into an adorable heart.

DIRECTIONS

Defrost the puff pastry for about 45 minutes according to the package directions.

Preheat oven to 400 degrees and line baking sheet with parchment paper.

Sprinkle a little white sugar on surface area and place thawed pastry on top. Use a rolling pin and roll out the pastry into a thinner and longer rectangle.

Sprinkle the rolled pastry dough with 1 tbsp of sugar and then top with a raspberry jam spreading it out evenly leaving an inch all around.

Roll half of the pastry dough in towards the center. Roll the other side towards the center. Repeat rolling each side until you have one long piece.

Place dough in the freezer for 15 mins to firm up and and cut into 1/2 inch slices.

Bake for 12-15 minutes or until golden brown.

INGREDIENTS

1 package of Puff Pastry Sheets

1/2 cup of Raspberry Preserves

Sugar for topping

SUGARED CRANBERY MINI CHEESCAKES TOPPED WITH *Raspberry* PRESERVES

READY IN 2 HOURS   SERVES **4-6**

INGREDIENTS

Crust
2/3 cup of graham cracker crumbs

1 ½ tablespoons of sugar

3 tablespoons of butter, melted

Pinch of salt

Topping
Raspberry Preserves

Filling
2 – 8oz containers of whipped cream cheese

1/2 cup of sugar

1 teaspoon of pure vanilla extract

2 large eggs – room temperature

1/4 cup of cup sour cream – room temperature

Pinch of salt

DIRECTIONS

Preheat oven to 325°F and place the rack in the center position. Line a muffin tin with 12 cupcake liners. Set aside.

For the crust - Combine the graham crumbs, 1 ½ tablespoons of sugar and melted butter in a bowl. Divide the mixture evenly among the muffin liners and press it down with the bottom with the back of a spoon. Set aside.

For the filling- Place the softened cream cheese in a large bowl and beat with a mixer on medium until creamy and smooth, about 1-2 minutes. Add sugar, salt and vanilla. Mix until thoroughly combined, with the mixer on medium low. Scrape the bowl to make sure it all combined well.

Add the eggs, one at a time, with the mixer on low, beating well after each addition. Scrape as needed. Add the sour cream and mix until incorporated. Give the bowl one last scrape to be sure the ingredients are thoroughly combined. Spoon the mixture evenly into the muffin tins over the crust.

Bake for about 18-20 minutes or until centers are almost set. The cheesecakes will rise during baking and are likely to crack a bit. Remove from the oven and set on a rack to cool completely. Chill the cheesecakes in the muffin tin for at least 2 hours or overnight, before removing from the tin and topping. The cheesecakes will sink in a bit after being chilled in the fridge. Fill with Raspberry preserves and top with sugared cranberries.

Raspberry BOURBON COCKTAIL

READY IN 10 MINS

SERVES 1

INGREDIENTS

2 Tablespoons of Raspberry Preserves

2 Tablespoons of Bourbon

1 Tablespoon of Triple Sec

3 Tablespoons of Orange Juice

1/2 of ice

Club soda, to top

Garnish with Orange Segment

DIRECTIONS

Add Bourbon, Triple Sec, Orange Juice, Raspberry Preserves and Ice to cocktail shaker.

Shake well. Pour into glass and fill with club soda. Garnish with a lemon segment.

Peach Preserve RECIPES

& BISCUITS

My mom made peach and pear preserves every summer when I was a kid. We would have jars of preserves in our pantry that we would enjoy throughout the year. I am thankful for those summers and everything she taught me about how to make homemade preserves.

BUTTERMILK BISCUITS TOPPED WITH *Peach* PRESERVES

Homemade buttermilk biscuits topped with Peach Preserves captures the essence of childhood. My mom would whip up a pan of homemade biscuits almost every weekend and serve them with her homemade peach or pear preserves.

DIRECTIONS

Preheat the oven to 450°F. In a medium bowl, use a sifter to sift the flour, baking powder and salt. Sifting the dry ingredients will make your biscuits really light and fluffy.

Create a well in your dry ingredients and add in the shortening using a fork and mix until mixture looks like fine crumbs. Stir in the buttermilk until mixture forms a soft dough and leaves the side of the bowl.

Put some extra flour on your hands and knead the dough a few times. Pinch off enough dough for the palm of your hand and roll into a ball and place on an ungreased baking sheet.

Once you have all the balls of biscuits on the baking sheet, dip your knuckles into flour and use the back of your hand to press down a bit on the biscuits.

Bake at 450 degrees until lightly browned. Serve with a tablespoon of Peach Preserves on top of warm biscuit.

INGREDIENTS

2 cups of all-purpose flour

3 teaspoons of baking powder

1 teaspoon of salt

1/2 cup of Crisco shortening

3/4 cup of buttermilk

READY IN 35 **MIN**
SERVES **4-6**

Peach JAM MUFFINS

READY IN 35 MIN   **SERVES 4-6**

Whip up a batch of these peach jam muffins as a starter for a large bunch or for a light breakfast and enjoy with a hot cup of coffee or tea.

DIRECTIONS

For the Muffins- In a large size bowl, whisk together the flour, baking powder, salt and sugar. In another large size bowl, lightly beat the eggs with an electric hand mixer, then beat in the milk, melted butter, and the vanilla extract.

Pour in the egg mixture. Stir gently with a wooden spoon or spatula just until combined. Do not overmix. Spoon one half of the batter into greased or paper-lined muffin trays. Add a heaping teaspoon of peach preserves to the center of each and then spoon in the remaining batter. Bake at 400° F for about 15 - 17 minutes until the muffins are golden brown.

For the topping- Melt the butter in a small bowl. After the muffins are baked, allow them to cool in the pan for about 5 minutes. Brush the tops with melted butter and sprinkle raw sugar on top. Serve muffins warm, or transfer them to a wire rack to cool completely.

INGREDIENTS

For the Muffins

3 cups all-purpose flour

1 1/2 tbsp. baking powder

1/8 tsp. salt

3/4 cup granulated sugar

3 eggs

1 1/2 cup milk (slightly warmed)

11 tablespoons of melted butter, cooled

1 1/2 tsp. vanilla extract

1/2 cup of Peach Preserves

For Topping

1/4 cup unsalted butter

1/4 cup of raw sugar

SPICY *Peach* BBQ SAUCE

READY IN 30 MIN   **SERVES 4-6**   

This BBQ Sauce is both tangy and sweet and amazing paired with grilled chicken wings. This recipe is a must have for your summer BBQ's.

DIRECTIONS

Combine tomato sauce, apple cider vinegar, brown sugar, honey, Worcestershire sauce, onion powder, garlic powder, salt, pepper, BBQ sauce and 1 cup of Peach Preserves in a medium saucepan and cook on medium heat.

Bring to simmer and then cook until thickened for 20 minutes.

Toss with grilled chicken wings in the sauce.

INGREDIENTS

1 cup of tomato sauce
1/4 cup of apple cider vinegar
1/4 cup of brown sugar
1.4 cup of honey
2 tablespoons of Worcestershire sauce
1/2 teaspoon of onion powder
1 teaspoon of garlic powder
1/2 teaspoon of kosher salt
1/8 teaspoon of black pepper
1/8 teaspoon of cayenne pepper
1/4 cup of Honey BBQ Sauce
1 cup of Peach Preserves

Peach COBBLER COCKTAIL

Peach Cobbler is a classic Southern dessert so why not turn it into a cocktail. This peach cobbler martini is a great dessert cocktail to complete any Southern meal.

READY IN 10 **MIN**

SERVES 1

DIRECTIONS

Spread Peach Preserves on to a small plate.

On a separate plate, add crushed graham crackers.

Dip the rim of a martini glass in the peach preserves and then into the crushed graham crackers.

Add vodka, hazelnut liquor, and peach nectar to a martini shaker filled with ice, shake well and strain into martini glass rimmed with crushed graham crackers.

Garnish with a fresh sprig of mint.

INGREDIENTS

Crushed Graham Crackers

1 tablespoon of Peach Preserves

1 1/4 oz of Whipped cream vodka

1/4 oz of Hazelnut liquor

1/3 cup of Peach Nectar

Garnish with fresh mint

ALL ABOUT THE JAM EXTRAS

Raspberry vinaigrette is so easy to make with jam. Add 1/3 cup of Raspberry Jam, 1/2 cup of red wine vinegar, 1/4 cup of olive oil, and 1/4 teaspoon of salt. Whisk until combined.

In order to make blackberry syrup out of blackberry jam, you simply need to add a splash of water to the jam in a small pan over medium heat. Whisk until smooth, adding more water as needed until you get a nice, syrupy consistency.

Homemade peach preserves ice cream is so easy to make when you use the no churn method. You only need a 14 oz can of condensed milk, 2 cups of cold heavy cream and a pinch of salt. Swirl in the peach preserves before freezing.

Cooking with love is like
food for the soul.

My fondest memories are the times that I shared with my mom in the kitchen. As a mother, I now want to build not only lifelong memories with my daughter but also pass down recipes and cooking techniques that I learned from my mom.

THANK YOU

I hope that my recipes have shown you the many ways that you can incorporate jam into any dish or cocktail. I say all the time that there would be no "tea to spill" without my mom showing me how to can and make homemade preserves. Thank you Mama! I love you. Thank you Ebes Olumese for the amazing food photography.

If you have any suggestions or feedback, just drop me a note at spillingthesweettea@gmail.com. If you try one of the recipes, please tag me on social media!

Follow me @spilling_the_sweet_tea

FOOD ICONS

 CONTAINS **NUTS**

 MILDLY **SPICY**

PREP TIME: 30 MIN

SERVING SIZE: 4-6

LOW CARB FRIENDLY